play bass today!

T0079421

PLAYBACK+
Speed • Pitch • Balance • Loop

To access audio and video visit:
www.halleonard.com/mylibrary/proline
Enter Code
1737-5488-8376-4260

ISBN 978-1-5400-4575-1

Visit Hal Leonard Online at
www.halleonard.com

Contact us:
Hal Leonard
7777 West Bluemound Road
Milwaukee, WI 53213
Email: info@halleonard.com

In Europe, contact:
Hal Leonard Europe Limited
42 Wigmore Street
Marylebone, London, W1U 2RN
Email: info@halleonardeurope.com

In Australia, contact:
Hal Leonard Australia Pty. Ltd.
4 Lentara Court
Cheltenham, Victoria, 3192 Australia
Email: info@halleonard.com.au

Introduction

Track 1

Welcome to *Play Bass Today!*—the series designed to prepare you for any style of bass playing, from rock to blues to jazz to country. Whatever your taste in music, *Play Bass Today!* will give you the start you need.

About the Audio & Video

It's easy and fun to play bass, and the accompanying audio will make your learning even more enjoyable, as we take you step by step through each lesson and play each song along with a full band. Much like with a real lesson, the best way to learn this material is to read and practice a while first on your own, then listen to the audio. With *Play Bass Today!*, you can learn at your own pace. If there is ever something that you don't quite understand the first time through, go back to the track and listen again. Every musical track has been given a track number, so if you want to practice a song again, you can find it right away.

Some lessons in the book include video lessons, so you can see and hear the material being taught. Audio and videos are indicated with icons.

 Audio Icon    Video Icon

Contents

The Basics

Track 2

The Parts of the Bass

The bass is a great instrument—it holds down the bottom of the band, and it's easy and fun to play.

Although there are many different kinds of basses—including models with five, six, and even seven strings—the typical bass has four strings and all the parts shown to the right. Take some time to get acquainted with the parts of your bass.

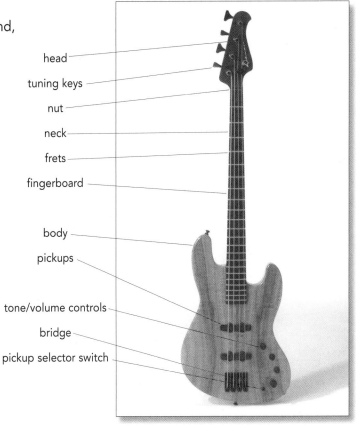

head
tuning keys
nut
neck
frets
fingerboard
body
pickups
tone/volume controls
bridge
pickup selector switch

How to Hold Your Bass

Sitting is probably the easiest position when first learning to play. Rest the bass on your right thigh and hold it against the right side of your chest, keeping your feet flat on the floor—or rest the bass on your left thigh and hold it against the center of your chest and slightly elevate your left leg. If you have a strap, you may prefer to stand. It is a good idea to start with a strap to find the most comfortable position for your bass.

The height and balance of your bass should be the same standing or sitting. Find a position that is comfortable for you—whatever position you choose, your hands must be free to move across the strings. Therefore, don't hold the bass with your hands; support it with your body or with a strap.

Your Right and Left Hands

You'll be playing your bass by plucking the strings with your right hand—using either your fingers or a pick. To play with your fingers, find a place to rest your thumb. Use your index and middle fingers to pluck the strings with an upward motion (toward your chest). To play with a pick, grip it between the thumb and index finger, keeping the rest of your hand relaxed and your fingers curved, and strike the strings in a downward motion. The fingers not holding the pick may rest on the bass for extra support.

Your left hand belongs on the neck of the bass. It, too, should be relaxed. To help you get a feel for the correct hand placement, follow these suggestions:

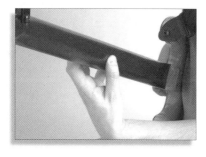

1. Place your thumb on the underside of the neck, positioned in the middle.

2. Arch your fingers so that you will be able to reach all the strings more easily.

3. Avoid letting the palm of your hand touch the neck of the bass.

Playing Is Easy

If you haven't already, try plucking the strings of your bass. Notice that some strings sound higher and some sound lower? Each has a different **pitch**. Pitch is the highness or lowness of a sound. On the bass, the strings are numbered 1 through 4, from the highest-sounding string (the thinnest) to the lowest-sounding one (the thickest).

You get different pitches from each bass string by pressing it down on various frets with the fingers of your left hand. Fretting higher up the neck produces sounds of a higher pitch; fretting lower on the neck produces sounds of a lower pitch. As you can see, the frets of the bass are also numbered, from low (near the head) to high (near the body).

The fingers of your left hand will also be numbered in this book, for convenience:

low ←→ high
STRINGS
④ ③ ② ①
FRETS:
1st
2nd
3rd
4th
5th

1st 2nd 3rd 4th

Tuning Up

If you loosen a string by turning its tuning key, the pitch will become lower; if you tighten the string, the pitch will become higher. When two pitches sound exactly the same, they are said to be *in tune*. There are many ways to get your bass in tune: you may use an electronic tuner, a piano, a pitch pipe, a tuning fork—you can even tune your bass purely to itself. For now, however, listen to the audio to help you tune your instrument. The bass's four open strings should be tuned to these pitches:

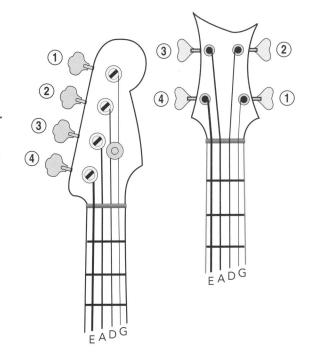

④ ③ ② ①
E–A–D–G
low ⟵⟶ high

Here are a few tips to help get you started:

- Whether tightening or loosening a string, turn the peg slowly so that you can concentrate on the changes in pitch. You may need to pick the string repeatedly to compare it.

- As you're tuning a string, you may notice that a series of pulsating **beat waves** becomes audible. These beat waves can actually help you tune: they'll slow down as you get closer to bringing two pitches together, and they'll stop completely once the two pitches are exactly the same.

- Instead of tuning a string *down* to pitch, tune it *up.* Tuning up allows you to stretch the string into place, which will help it stay in tune longer. So, if you begin with a string that is too high in pitch, tune it down first, and then bring it back up to pitch.

Another Way to Tune Your Bass

This is a great way to check your tuning or, if you don't have a pitch source, to tune your bass to itself.

1. Tune the 4th string E to a piano, a pitch pipe, an electronic tuner, or the track. If none of these are available, approximate E the best you can.
2. Press the 4th string at the 5th fret. This is A. Tune the open 3rd string to this pitch.
3. Press the 3rd string at the 5th fret. This is D. Tune the open 2nd string to this pitch.
4. Press the 2nd string at the 5th fret. This is G. Tune the open 1st string to this pitch.

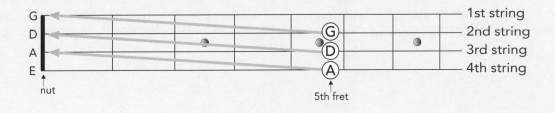

How to Read Music

Musical sounds are indicated by symbols called **notes.** Notes come in all shapes and sizes, but every note has two important components: pitch and rhythm.

Pitch

Pitch (the highness or lowness of a note) is indicated by the placement of the note on a **staff**, a set of five lines and four spaces. Notes higher on the staff are higher in pitch; notes lower on the staff are lower in pitch.

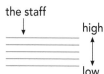

To name the notes on the staff, we use the first seven letters of the alphabet: **A–B–C–D–E–F–G**. Adding a **bass clef** assigns a particular note name to each line and space on the staff, centered on the pitch F, the fourth line from the bottom. In the bass clef, in which most music for the electric bass is written, the names of the lines, starting with the first line, are G, B, D, F, and A. The names of the spaces, starting with the first space, are A, C, E, and G.

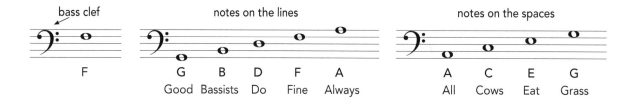

Rhythm

Rhythm refers to how long, or for how many beats, a note lasts. This is indicated with the following symbols:

o	♩	♩
whole note	half note	quarter note
(four beats)	*(two beats)*	*(one beat)*

To help you keep track of the beats in a piece of music, the staff is divided into **measures** (or "bars"). A **time signature** (or "meter") at the beginning of the staff indicates how many beats you can expect to find in each measure.

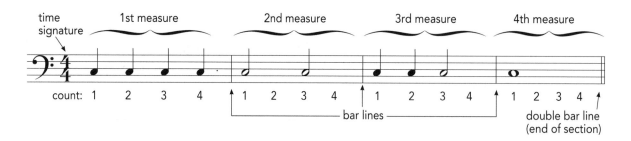

4/4 is perhaps the most common time signature. The top number ("4") tells you how many beats there are in each measure; the bottom number ("4") tells you what type of note value receives one beat. In 4/4 time, there are four beats in each measure, and each beat is worth one quarter note.

Intervals

The smallest distance, or interval, between two notes is called a **half step**. If you play any note on the bass and then play another note one fret higher or lower, you have just played a half step. If you move two frets higher (two half steps up) or two frets lower (two half steps down), you have moved one **whole step**.

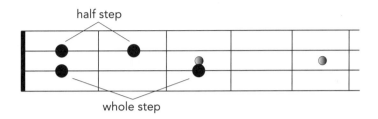

Accidentals

Any note can be raised or lowered a half step by placing an **accidental** directly before it.

Sharp (♯)   ⟶   Raises a note one half step (one fret)

Flat (♭)   ⟶   Lowers a note one half step (one fret)

Natural (♮) ⟶ Cancels previously used sharp or flat

Ledger Lines

Notes higher or lower than the range of the staff must be written using **ledger lines**. Ledger lines can be used above or below the staff.

Lesson 2 — The First String: G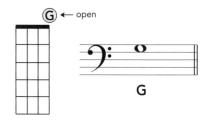

The first three notes we'll learn on the bass are all found on the highest (and thinnest) string. This is the first string, also called the G string.

G

■ Your first note, G, is an "open-string" tone. There's nothing to fret—simply pluck the open first string.

A

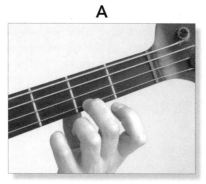

► Notice that your finger actually belongs *directly behind* each metal fret. If you place it on top of the fret, or too far back, you'll have difficulty getting a full, clear sound.

■ For the next note A, place your second finger on the second fret, and pluck the string.

B

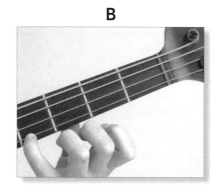

■ To play the note B, place your fourth finger on the fourth fret, and pluck the string.

Learn to recognize these notes both on the fretboard *and* on the staff. Then, when you're comfortable playing the notes individually, try this short exercise. Speak the note names aloud as you play (e.g., "G, A, B, A...").

Track 5

G-A-B

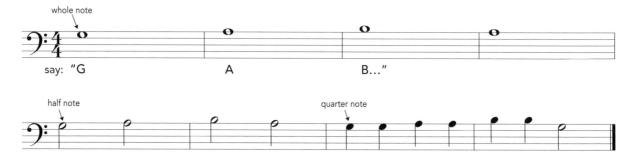

8

Of course, the best way to really learn these notes is to use them in some tunes. So let's do it. Start slowly with the following melodies, and keep your pace nice and even.

First Song

Track 6

Keeping Time

Having trouble keeping a steady rhythm? Try *tapping* and *counting* along with each song. If the bass is resting on your right leg, use your left foot to tap. Each time the foot comes down marks one beat. In 4/4 time, tap your foot four times in each measure, and count "1, 2, 3, 4." The first beat of each measure should be accented slightly—this is indicated below by the symbol ">."

count and tap: 1   2   3   4   1   2   3   4   1   2   3   4   1   2   3   4

Second Song

Track 7

► If you like, read through each song *without* your bass first: Tap the beat with your foot, count out loud, and *clap* through the rhythms.

Third Song

Track 8

Two New Notes: G♯ and B♭

Notice that we skipped the first and third frets? Let's go back and grab those notes.

G♯

▶ Remember sharps (♯) and flats (♭)? If not, review page 7.

■ To play the note G♯, place your first finger on the first fret.

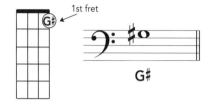

B♭

■ To play the note B♭, place your third finger on the third fret.

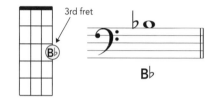

Let's try these new notes in a song.

Track 9

G♯-B♭

▶ Sharps and flats apply throughout the measure in which they appear.

Track 10

Play It!

Now here are some tunes to practice all five notes you've learned so far. Don't be afraid to review G, A, and B again before tackling these!

Track 11

Mix It Up

▶ Remember: A natural sign (♮) cancels a previous sharp or flat.

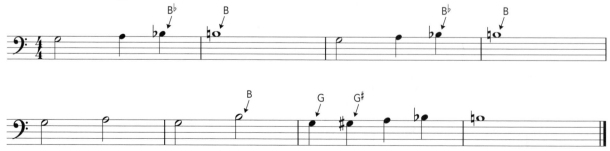

10

Mix It Down

Technique

Now we'll take a look at our left and right hand positions.

The Left Hand

Be sure to keep your left hand fingers curved but relaxed, and use just your fingertips to fret the notes. In this next exercise, try to keep your fingers down when you are finished fretting a note; when you are done, all your fingers should be touching the first string. Place your thumb on the back of the neck adjacent to your second finger. Keep your touch light.

keep fingers down

The Right Hand

If you're using your fingers to pluck the strings, alternate back and forth: index then middle. Keep your fingers close to the string so you are able to strike the string cleanly and precisely. If you're using a pick, strike the strings with a downward motion—remember, you are only going to play with the point of the pick, not the body.

The Second String: D

Track 14

Your next three notes are all played on the second string, D. You might want to check your tuning on that string before going any further.

D

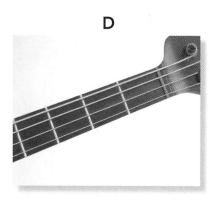

■ To play the note D, just pluck the open second string.

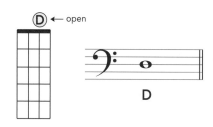

E

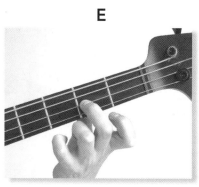

■ To play the note E, place your second finger at the second fret.

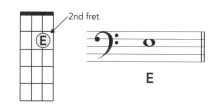

F

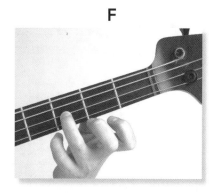

■ To play the note F, place your third finger at the third fret.

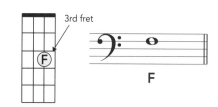

Practice these next exercises several times, slow and easy. Then play them along with the audio. Again, say the note names aloud, or think them, as you play.

Track 15

D-E-F

say or think : "D   E   F..."

Three-Note Groove

▶ Try to keep your eyes on the page, instead of on your bass.

Now here are some songs to practice *all* the notes you've learned so far on the first and second strings.

Track 17

Two-String Rock

Keep It Clean

To keep your bass lines sounding clean and punchy, try the following:

• If you're plucking the strings with your fingers, let each finger follow through to the next string after it plucks, allowing the lower string to stop your finger's motion. This does two things: 1) it mutes the lower string, keeping it from ringing, and 2) it controls how far your fingers move, increasing your right hand accuracy.

• If you're playing with a pick, allow the side of your thumb to lightly touch any lower strings as you pick; this will mute those strings, preventing them from ringing.

Track 18

That's Right

▶ Watch that jump from A to E (both played by the second finger). Try to keep it smooth.

Introducing Rests

In addition to notes, songs may also contain silences, or **rests**—beats in which you play nothing at all. A rest is a musical pause. Rests are like notes in that they have their own rhythmic values, instructing you how long (or for how many beats) to pause:

whole rest	half rest	quarter rest
(four beats)	*(two beats)*	*(one beat)*

You'll definitely want to stop any previous notes from ringing during a rest. To do this, try the following:

- After an open-string note, like G, touch the string lightly with your left-hand finger(s).

- After a fretted note, like F, decrease the pressure of your left-hand finger on the string.

Track 19

Rest Easy

Track 20

Rock 'n' Rest

Introducing the Pickup

Instead of starting a song with a rest, a **pickup measure** may be used. A pickup measure is an incomplete measure that deletes any opening rests. So, if a pickup has only one beat, you count "1, 2, 3" and start playing on beat 4.

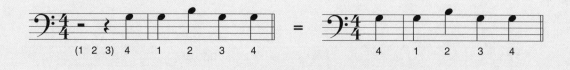

Two New Notes: E♭ and F♯

Notice that we skipped the first and fourth frets on the D string? Let's go back and grab 'em.

E♭

► Remember: E♭ is one fret *lower* than E. F♯ is one fret *higher* than F.

■ To play the note E♭, place your first finger at the first fret.

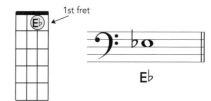

F♯

■ To play the note F♯, place your fourth finger at the fourth fret.

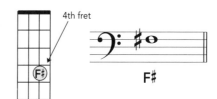

Now let's try these new notes.

Track 21

E♭-F♯

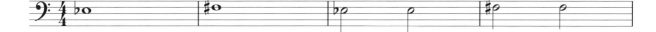

Track 22

My Pickup's Got a Flat!

► Notice the pickup measure here. You actually begin playing on beat 4.

Track 23

Mixin' It Up Again

Two-String Review

Here's all the notes we've learned so far, from D to B. That's ten notes in all!

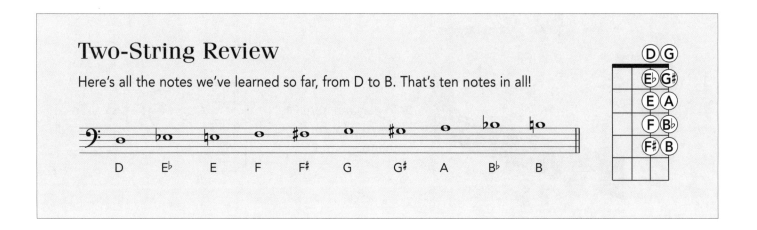

D E♭ E F F♯ G G♯ A B♭ B

Track 24

Review This!

Track 25

Walk Away

► Use your left-hand technique here (à la page 11).

The Third String: A

Track 26

Are you ready to move ahead? Then it's time for another string. Your new notes, A, B, and C, are all played on the third string.

A

► Notice we're using the same fret positions as on the second string: open, 2nd, and 3rd.

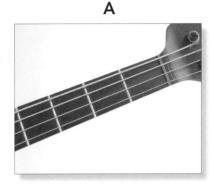

■ To play the note A, pluck the open third string.

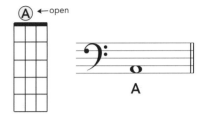

B

■ To play the note B, place your second finger at the second fret.

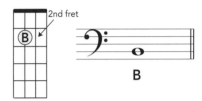

C

■ To play the note C, place your third finger at the third fret.

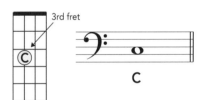

Track 27

A-B-C

say or think: "A   B   C..."

A-B-C Soup

► Be sure to mute the strings during rests.

Tempo is the speed at which a song is played—from very slow to very fast. For now, try to play at a tempo that allows your eyes to read ahead of the music; this'll give your fingers time to prepare for each note. As you become more confident with the notes, you'll naturally speed up.

Brother

Introducing Octaves

If your new A and B sound familiar, they should. They sound much like the A and B on the first string, but they're an "octave" lower. The word **octave** means "eight notes apart." (You'll understand that more a bit later…) Bass players use octaves a lot—the notes of an octave are almost interchangeable, and they can really "fatten up" a bass line—so get used to this new concept.

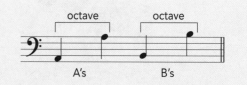

Big Rock

► You can let the strings ring here; octaves sound good that way.

Two New Notes: B♭ and C♯

Did you think we'd skip the first and fourth frets on the A string? Not a chance!

B♭

■ To play the note B♭, place your first finger on the first fret.

■ To play the note C♯, place your fourth finger at the fourth fret.

C♯

Now let's put these notes to good use.

Track 31

B♭-C♯

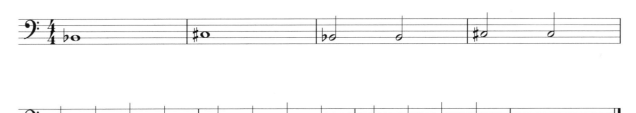

Blues Baby!

Track 32

Introducing Eighth Notes

If you divide a quarter note in half, what you get is an **eighth note**.
An eighth note looks like a quarter note, but with a flag on it.

Two eighth notes equal one quarter note. To help you keep track of the beat, consecutive eighths
are connected with a beam.

To count eighth notes, divide the beat into two, and use "and" between the beats. Practice this,
first by counting out loud while tapping your foot on the beat, and then by playing the notes while
counting and tapping.

Eighth rests are the same, but you pause instead of playing.

Now, try some songs that use eighth notes. Keep that foot tapping!

Track 33

Eighth-Note Rock

► Keep letting your right hand fingers follow through after plucking the strings.

Alternate Picking

If you're using a pick to play these eighth-note lines, try them with *alternate picking*. This is one way
to add speed and facility to your bass playing. Alternate picking is a combination of downstrokes (⊓)
on the beat (on "1," "2," "3," or "4") and upstrokes (∨) off the beat (on the "ands"). This short exercise on your open A string will give you a better idea of how it's done:

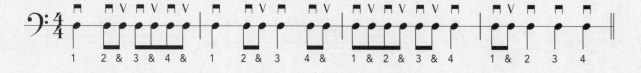

Blues By Eight

► Try this song both ways: first with all downstrokes, then with alternate picking.

3/4 Time

The next song is in **3/4** meter. That is, three beats (quarter notes) per measure.

three beats per measure
quarter note (1/4) gets one beat

count: 1 2 3   1 2 3   1 2 3   1 2 3

3/4 time feels very different from 4/4 time. Be sure to accent the first beat of each measure, just slightly; this will help you feel the new meter.

Amazing Grace

► Notice the pickup measure. The melody begins on beat 3 while the bass rests.

FYI: It's usually the bassist's job to lay down the foundation of a song while other instruments play the melody. The above bass line is a great example of that. (For a real challenge, try singing the melody at the same time that you play your bass part!)

Mr. Three

Repeat signs (𝄆▬▬▬▬▬▬𝄇) tell you to repeat everything in between them. If only one sign appears (:𝄀), repeat from the beginning of the piece.

Track 37

Four and Repeat

Track 38

Three and Repeat

► This song has a "new" note, D♯.

D♯ is a really old note with a new name. You already know it as E♭. How can one note have two names? It just depends on which way you approach it, from E or D. Notes like D♯ and E♭ are called **enharmonic equivalents**—a fancy way of saying "two names for the same pitch."

The Fourth String: E

Track 39

The notes E, F, and G are played on the fourth string of the bass. As you practice these new notes, memorize their positions on the staff and ledger lines. You'll definitely use them a lot!

E

■ To play the note E, pluck the open fourth string.

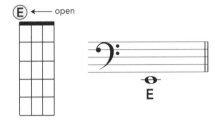

F

■ To play the note F, place your first finger at the first fret.

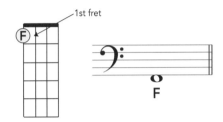

G

■ To play the note G, place your third finger at the third fret.

This is it—the last string!

Track 40

E-F-G

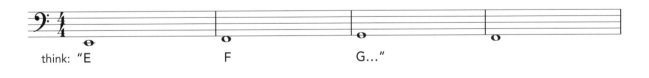

think: "E   F   G..."

Don't forget to let your eyes read a little ahead while you play.

Track 41

Fourth-String Strut

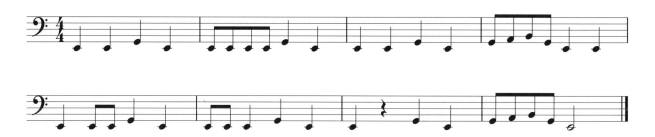

Track 42

Bass Rock

Ties and Dots

The *tie* is a curved line that connects two notes of the same pitch. When you see a tie, play the first note and then hold it for the total value of both notes.

1   2   3   (4   1)   2   3   (4   1   2)   3   4

Ties are useful when you need to extend the value of a note across a bar line.

Another way to extend the value of a note is to use a **dot**. A dot extends any note by one-half its value. Most common is the dotted half note:

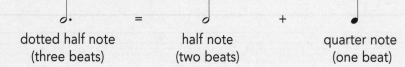

dotted half note   =   half note   +   quarter note
(three beats)   (two beats)   (one beat)

You'll encounter the dotted half note in many songs, especially those that use 3/4 meter.

Tongue-Tied

Mr. Ballad

► Watch that third-finger jump (from G to C). Make it smooth.

Two More Notes: F♯ and G♯

From the strings that we already know, let's add two more new notes: F♯ and G♯.

F♯

■ To play the note F♯, place your second finger at the second fret.

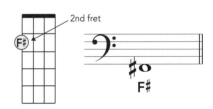

G♯

■ To play the note G♯, place your fourth finger at the fourth fret.

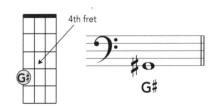

F♯–G♯

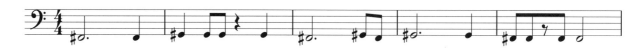

Low Groove

► There's that D♯ again!

Blues in E

Steppin' Out

The Dotted Quarter Note

As we know, a dot lengthens a note by one half its time value. When a quarter note is followed by a dot, its time value is increased from 1 beat to 1 1/2 beats.

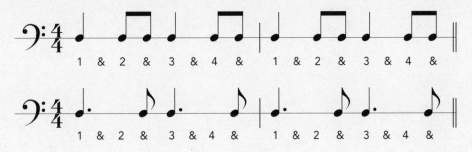

A dotted quarter note is usually followed by an eighth note. This pattern has a total time value of two beats.

To get more comfortable with counting dotted quarter notes, try the following rhythm exercise:

Rockin' Riff

Track 49

▶ The word *riff* is slang for a repeated instrumental figure, or musical idea.

Bossa #1

Track 50

First Position Review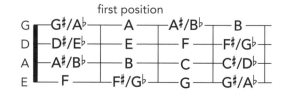

Track 51

We've covered all four strings, but let's double back and review the notes we've learned. This area of the bass neck—from the open strings to fret 4—is called **first position**.

first position

G	G#/Ab	A	A#/Bb	B
D	D#/Eb	E	F	F#/Gb
A	A#/Bb	B	C	C#/Db
E	F	F#/Gb	G	G#/Ab

Again, notes that have different names but occupy the same fret (like F# and Gb) are referred to as **enharmonic equivalents**. Either note name is acceptable.

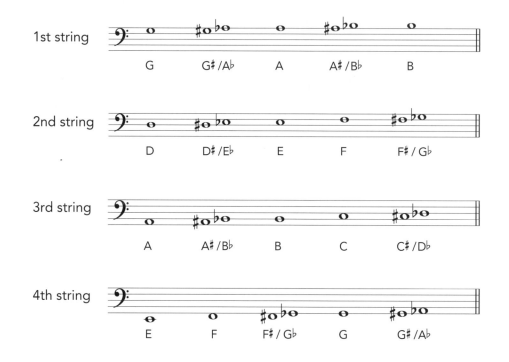

In case you haven't noticed, when we play in first position, each finger gets assigned to one fret—first finger to the first fret, second finger to the second fret, third finger to the third fret, and fourth finger to the fourth fret. This is called the **one-finger-per-fret** rule. This way, we can easily cover all the notes in first position without having to shift hand position, and we always know how to finger each note.

Track 52

One-Finger-Per Fret Rock

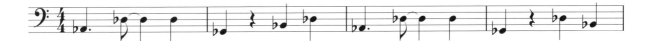

New Flats

Staccato

If you see a dot (•) above or below a note, it means to play the note short, a.k.a. **staccato**. To do this, release pressure on the note with your left-hand finger, or mute the note if it's an open string.

Funky

staccato

Punky

More Octaves

Technique

We'll take a look at our left and right hands again.

The Left Hand

Try this exercise. Remember to keep your fingers down as you play each note.

The Right Hand

Now we will practice skipping strings. Notice that every other measure is played staccato. Pay close attention to your right hand to keep the strings from ringing. Go very slowly!

Mr. Technique

2/2 Time

In **2/2 time**, there are two beats per measure, and the half note gets the beat. This actually feels a lot like 4/4, but you only tap your foot twice in each measure.

Two for Espresso

Hail to the Bassist

Notes at the Fifth Fret

Track 61

Before we move on to some new topics, let's grab a few more notes up higher on the fretboard. These are all found at the fifth fret and should be played with your fourth (pinky) finger.

A

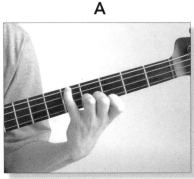

■ To play the note A, place your fourth finger at the fifth fret of the *fourth* string.

4th string

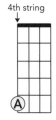

A

D

■ To play the note D, place your fourth finger at the fifth fret of the *third* string.

3rd string

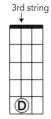

D

G

■ To play the note G, place your fourth finger at the fifth fret of the *second* string.

2nd string

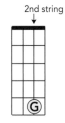

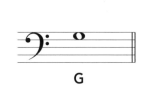

G

C

■ To play the note C, place your fourth finger at the fifth fret of the *first* string.

1st string

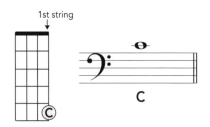

C

You'll probably want to move your hand up the fretboard, just a bit, to reach that fifth fret...

Introducing Second Position

It's easier to play notes at the fifth fret if you move your hand up the neck to *second position*. In second position, your first finger moves up to the *second fret*. The rest of your fingers fall into place on the adjacent frets (following the one-finger-per-fret rule).

Track 62

► Play this in second position, using just your pinky.

Fifth-Fret Warrior

Of course, the new note here is the high C, so let's take advantage of it.

Track 63

Hittin' the High C

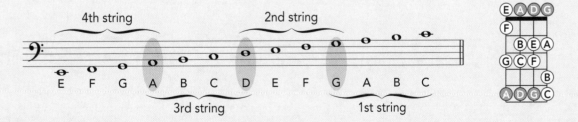

There's More Than One Place To Find a Note!

The more you play bass, the more you'll discover there's more than one place to find the same note. For instance, we now have two places to play the notes A, D, and G.

Which fingering you choose depends on:

- *Where your fingers are.* Are you in first position? Second position?
- *What sound you prefer.* Open strings have a different sound than fretted notes.

Introducing Tablature or "Tab"

From now on, we'll be seeing a new type of musical notation called **tablature**, or **"tab"** for short. It consists of four lines, one for each string of your bass. The numbers written on the lines indicate which fret to play in order to sound the correct notes.

E	B	F♯	C
(string 4, open)	(string 3, fret 2)	(string 2, fret 4)	(string 1, fret 5)

Tab is a very popular notation method for bass music and can be used to show finger patterns and positions on the neck. Refer to it when you need clarification on where to play a note. Otherwise, keep reading the notes on the staff.

Track 64

Tab This!

► This song plays well in second position. (Notice the tab.)

Track 65

Tab That!

► Try this riff in first position, then in second, as indicated.

Lesson 8 Major Scales

Now that you've got a handle on all four strings up to the fifth fret, it's time to start learning about scales. "What's a scale?" you ask. A **scale** is an arrangement of notes in a specific, sequential pattern. Most scales use eight notes, with the top and bottom notes being an octave apart.

Two things give a scale its name: its lowest note (called the **root**) and the pattern of whole and half steps it uses. A **major** scale is always built using this interval formula:

whole – whole – half – whole – whole – whole – half

Remember: On the bass, a whole step is two frets, a half step is one fret. Let's take a look!

E Major

Track 66

▶ Notice that in an E major scale, there are four sharps: F#, G#, C#, and D#.

F Major

Track 67

▶ Notice that in an F major scale, there is one flat: B♭.

G Major

Track 68

▶ Notice that in a G major scale, there is one sharp: F#.

Key Signatures

In written music, a **key signature** is found at the beginning of the staff, between the clef and the time signature. It defines what notes will be sharp or flat—or essentially, what key you'll be playing in.

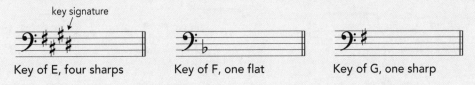

Key of E, four sharps   Key of F, one flat   Key of G, one sharp

So What's a Key?

Good question. Key and scale are almost the same thing. When we know a scale—like E major—we have all the notes we need to play in the corresponding key—like E major!

Like scales, keys have two components:

- a root, or **tonic**, which is the defining note. This is often (but not always) the first or last note in a piece of music, and it usually feels the most resolved, or "at rest."

- a **quality**. In this case, major.

Just remember, to play in a key, use the notes of the scale with the same name. For example, to play in the key of E major, use the notes of an E major scale. To play in G major, use the notes of a G major scale.

Track 69

E Jam

► Watch the key signature. It tells you what notes to play sharp (or flat) in the music.

Track 70

Unplugged in G

Track 71

Descent in F

36

Name That Key!

More Major Scales

Now, we'll take a look at some more major scales! Notice that major scales (and keys) contain either sharps *or* flats—but never both.

A Major

► A major has three sharps: C♯, F♯, and G♯.

B♭ Major

► B♭ major has two flats: B♭ and E♭.

Here is a good one for second position.

C Major

► C major is a popular scale—it has no sharps or flats.

Lesson 9 | Minor Scales

Since we just learned six major scales, let's even things out by learning some *minor* scales. A minor scale is built like this:

whole – half – whole – whole – half – whole – whole

Wow, what was that? Let's take a closer look!

Track 76

E Minor

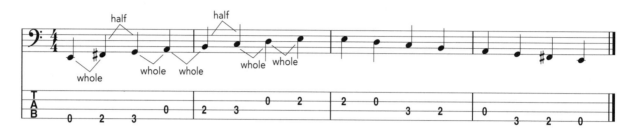

Track 77

F Minor

Track 78

G Minor

Major vs. Minor

The difference between major and minor scales is not just about whole and half steps—it's about how they **sound.** Take a minute to compare a major and a minor scale—like G major and G minor. Notice how each makes you feel? It's difficult to put into words, but generally we say that major scales (and keys) have a strong, upbeat, or happy quality, while minor scales and keys have a darker, sadder quality.

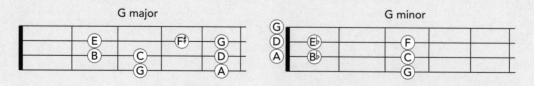

Minor scales have key signatures, too. But we'll explore those in Lesson 15. For now, let's try some songs in minor keys.

Rage in E Minor

tonic

Sad Story

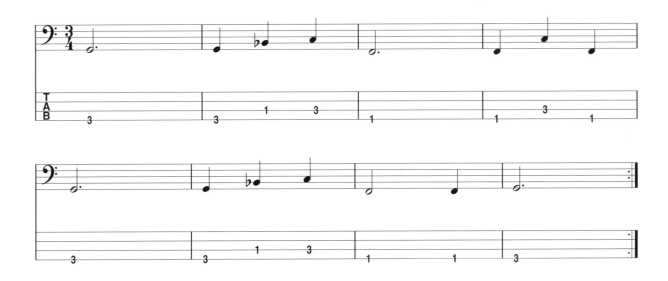

Why?

Hammer-Ons and Pull-Offs

The hammer-on and pull-off are great techniques for building speed and improving your left hand coordination—and they sound cool.

1. To play a **hammer-on**, place your first finger on the B♭ shown. Pluck the note, and then "hammer down" with your third finger onto the second note, C. The force of that finger fretting the string causes the note to sound (without plucking).

2. To play a **pull-off**, start with both fingers planted on their notes. Pluck the note C, then "pull off" with your third finger, letting the note B♭ sound. Got it?

Track 82

Hammer Head

► Use your first and third fingers for this. Then try your second and fourth fingers.

Track 83

Pull My Finger!

Track 84

Combo Platter

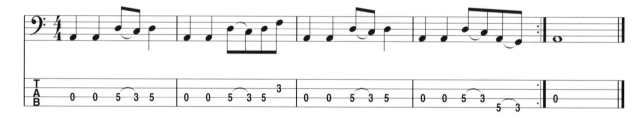

40

More Minor Scales

Let's add some more minor scales to our vocabulary.

Track 85

A Minor

► A minor has no sharps or flats—like C major!

Track 86

B♭ Minor

Track 87

C Minor

► This one requires a bit of a stretch on the top string.

Name That Key, Pt. 2

Is it major or is it minor? Listen for the quality, and find the tonic note.

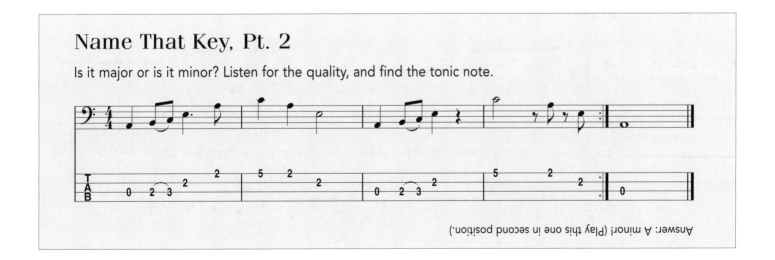

Answer: A minor! (Play this one in second position.)

41

Style

Finally, let's put to use all that we've learned. In this lesson, we will play through some common styles of music. Roll up your sleeves, and let's go!

Track 88

'50s Rock

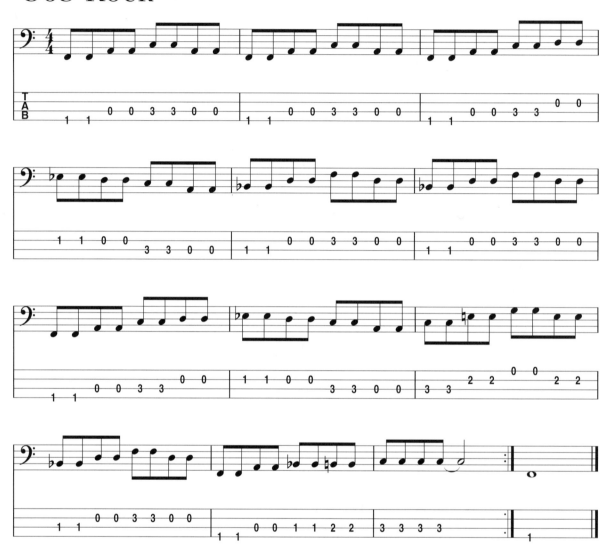

Track 89

Hard Rock

► This one plays well in second position.

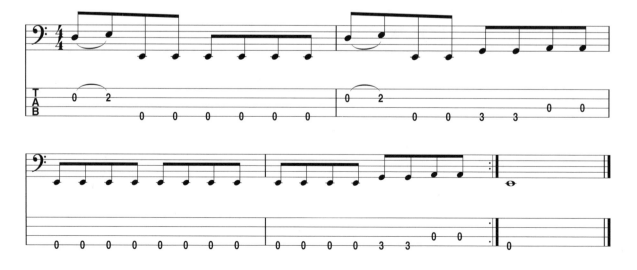

Alternative Rock

Rap Metal

Pop Rock

Pop Ballad

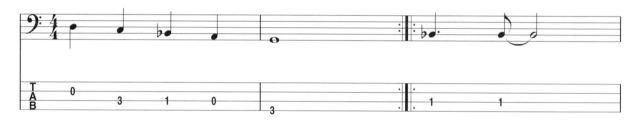

R&B

► This song uses a multi-measure rest. The bass waits four measures, then begins playing.

Track 95

Reggae

► Play this one in second position—you'll have to stretch to reach the low F.

Track 96

Funk

Track 97

Jazz

Bossa #2

Country

► This one requires a position shift. Also, to play the same fret on adjacent strings, try "rolling" your finger across.

First and Second Position

Track 100

Let's take some time to review the notes we've learned so far. **First position** is the area of the bass neck from the open strings to fret 4. **Second position** is the area from the second to the fifth fret.

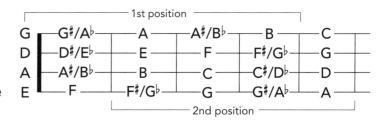

Remember: Notes like F♯ and G♭ are called **enharmonic equivalents**—two different note names for the same pitch. Either spelling is acceptable. There is no difference in the way these two notes are played or in the way they sound.

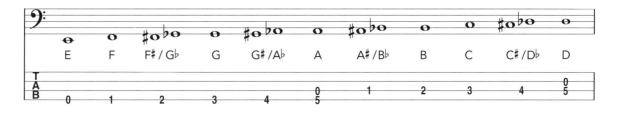

When playing in a position, we generally follow the **one-finger-per-fret-rule**—first finger on the first fret, second finger on the second fret, third finger on the third fret, and fourth finger on the fourth fret. That describes the first position. If you need to reach the fifth fret, move your hand to second position—with your first finger on the second fret and your pinky on the fifth fret.

first position

second position

Let's try some bass lines using the notes in first and second position.

Position One

Position Two

Reminder: If you see a dot (·) above or below a note, it means to play the note short, or **staccato**. To do this, release pressure on the fret—or if it's an open string, touch it lightly—with your left-hand finger.

Stuck At Zero

► Practice this slowly to make sure each note is staccato.

By the way, if you're plucking the strings with your fingers, be sure to alternate consistently back and forth between your index and middle finger. If you're playing with a pick, use either all downstrokes or alternate picking (downstrokes and upstrokes).

Metronome

A **metronome** is a device used to mark time. Practicing with a metronome forces us to listen to a consistent beat (or click) and match it. The tempo, or rate, of the click is measured in **bpm's**—beats per minute. Metronome practice improves consistency, listening, and matching skills.

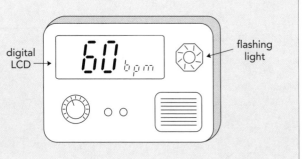

digital LCD →

flashing light

Track 104

Practicing with a Metronome

Let's try practicing with a metronome. We'll place the metronome click on different beats within the same example.

Metronome on beats 1, 2, 3, and 4.

Metronome on beats 1 and 3.

Metronome on beats 2 and 4.

► This one's a little tricky, so take it slowly.

Now we'll play along with the whole band to a *click track*—which is basically a metronome used when recording a band. The click track will be on beats 1, 2, 3, and 4.

Track 105

Seesaw

The click track will be on beats 1 and 3.

Track 106

Boots

► Count beats 2 and 4 silently.

49

Movable Scale Forms

Track 107

In Lessons 8 and 9, we talked about major and minor scales, and how we can use them to play in keys. We also discovered that some scale shapes are movable. Just find the desired root note (on strings 3 or 4) then apply the pattern of your choice—and there's your scale!

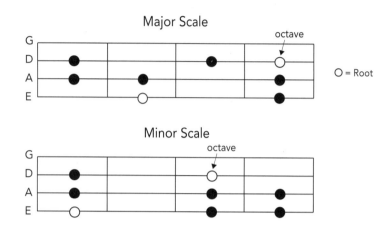

Let's try moving these scale forms around a bit so you can see how they work. First, we'll use the major shape—play a C major scale, then move down a half step to play a B major scale. Then we'll try the minor shape—play an F♯ minor scale followed by B♭ minor.

Track 108

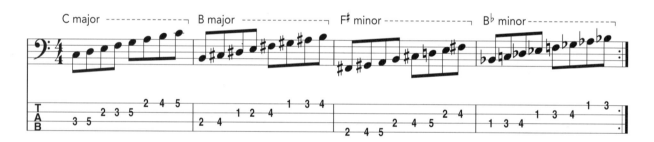

You've just played four scales using only two shapes! The beauty of these shapes is that you don't have to think of them only in block form. Let's look deeper and break them down by string.

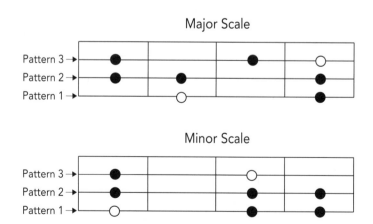

Scales on a Single String

Let's try a G major scale *on one string*—using the patterns we just broke down. Here's how we do it: Play the first string pattern, then skip one fret (one whole step); then play the second string pattern, skip one fret (one whole step); then play the third string pattern. We'll be moving up the neck into some uncharted territory, so pay close attention.

G Major

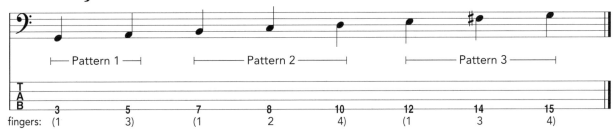

Now we'll try this same approach with the G minor scale.

G Minor

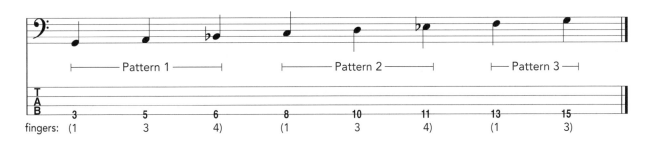

Now, let's try a C major scale on one string. Keep the same fingers playing the same notes as you do when you play the scale normally; except for the first string pattern—use your first and third fingers (see below).

C Major

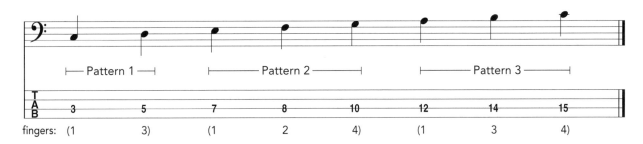

Now try C minor.

C Minor

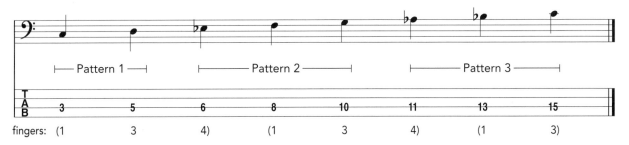

Now we'll play some songs moving up and down the neck using these patterns, so you can see their practical use. Again we'll be moving up the neck of the bass—to notes and positions you might not be familiar with—so pay close attention to the tablature. This is a great way to learn those notes! This song uses octaves up high on the neck.

Bee C's

Track 110

► Pay close attention to notes and shapes on the A string.

*C major scale.

Octaver

Track 111

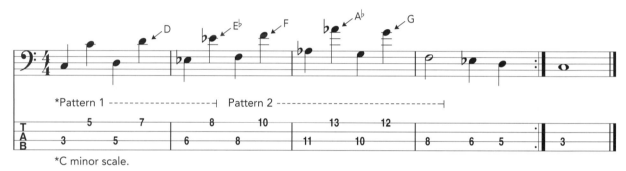

*C minor scale.

Sixteenth Notes and Rests

Sixteenth notes look like eighth notes, but they have two flags or beams:

Sixteenth rests also have two flags:

Two sixteenths equal one eighth. Four sixteenths equal one quarter. Here's a diagram showing the relationship of sixteenth notes to all the rhythmic values you've learned:

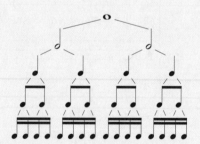

To help you keep track of the beat, consecutive sixteenth notes are connected with a beam. To count sixteenths, divide the beat into four, and count "1-e-&-a, 2-e-&-a, 3-e-&-a, 4-e-&-a":

1 e & a 2 e & a 3 e & a 4 e & a

Because sixteenth notes move so quickly, you'll find them easier to play if you alternate between your index and middle finger when plucking the strings. If you use a pick, try alternating down-strokes (⊓) with upstrokes (∨).

Alternate Sixteenths

Punk Sixteenths

Now try some sixteenth rests; this gets a little tricky, so go slow—and don't forget to count. (The first time through this, concentrate on counting; the second time, watch what your right hand is doing, and compare it to what's shown.)

Rest Up

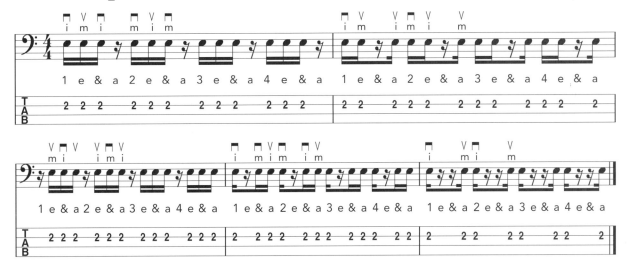

Brake Fluid

Fifth Position

So far, we've learned to read in the first and second position of the bass, and we've explored up the neck using movable scale forms—skills that will serve us well in many situations. Now let's expand our horizons by learning to read in a new area: the *fifth position*.

■ Fifth position starts on high C at the 5th fret—this time played with the index finger.

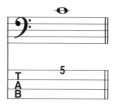

Starting at the 5th fret allows us to access several more notes on the G string that weren't available to us in the first and second position. Of course, it also gives new fingerings for many familiar notes. Playing in this position can help us create smoother, more consistent bass lines.

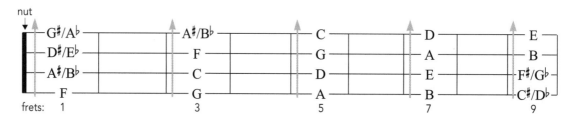

You may notice that, since we no longer have the open strings working for us, we sometimes have to cover more frets—in general, follow the one-finger-per-fret rule, but allow your pinky to cover both the 8th and 9th frets.

► Say the notes aloud as you play them.

Fifth Position

To get a better feel for this position, try a few scales and songs. This first scale can be played in first position or fifth, so try it both ways.

A Minor

Track 119

Rhythmic

► Make sure to alternate fingers when plucking with the right hand.

Now try this E♭ major scale.

Track 120

E♭ Major

Track 121

Mother Earth

Combining Sixteenths with Eighths

Now we're going to start combining sixteenth notes and eighth notes over the same beat. This can get a bit confusing, so take it slow and don't forget to count.

Track 122

Eighth & Two Sixteenths

Two Sixteenths & an Eighth

Sixteenth, Eighth, Sixteenth

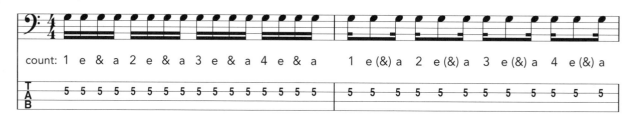

Remember: A **dot** adds half the value to a note. So, in this case, a dotted eighth note equals three sixteenth notes, or an eighth plus a sixteenth.

Dotted Eighth & Sixteenth

► Take this one
slowly and be
sure to count.

Sixteenth & Dotted Eighth

This song uses more than one position.

Funky Feel

► Shift your left hand when moving to a new position.

Sometimes, you'll use more than one position to play a song. For instance, you might start in open position, then move up to fifth position for some higher notes, and then move back down again. If there's no tablature, survey the song before playing it to determine what positions to use.

Switch Position

Memorizing Notes

Learning the location of all the notes on your bass is essential. Here's a good way to practice memorizing them. We'll start by naming the notes vertically on the first fret: F–A♯/B♭–D♯/E♭–G♯/A♭. Then the third fret: G–C–F–A♯/B♭. Now continue up the neck naming notes on the fifth, seventh, and ninth frets. This is a fast way to learn all your notes. Every time you pick up your bass, do this exercise; you'll be surprised at how fast you'll know your bass neck.

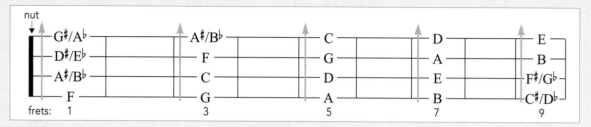

When you conquer the first, third, fifth, seventh, and ninth frets, move on to the second, fourth, sixth, and eighth frets. They should be easy because you'll already know the notes next to them!

When you know fifth position well enough, try some new songs, like these!

Track 129

Upside Your Head

▶ Be warned: there are some pinky stretches here!

Track 130

Tongue in Cheek

Lesson 14 | Intervals

Track 131

An *interval* is the term for the distance between two notes. In Level 1, we looked at the intervals of a half step (one fret) and a whole step (two frets). Now we'll look at intervals in relation to scales and chords. Every interval has two parts to its name:

- **number**—second, third, fourth, fifth, sixth, etc.
- **quality**—major, minor, perfect, diminished, or augmented

Knowledge of intervals is essential to building great bass lines. For the next twelve examples, we'll play an interval, and then a song based around that interval—so you can hear what it sounds like. All examples will be in the key of C.

Minor Second

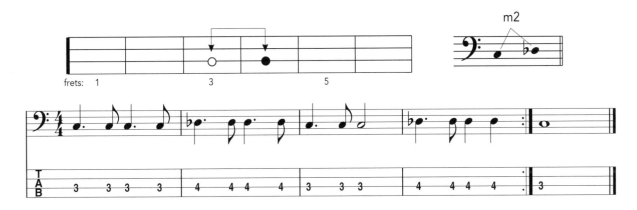

Track 132

Major Second

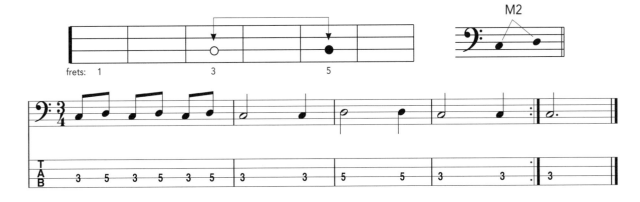

Track 133

Minor Third

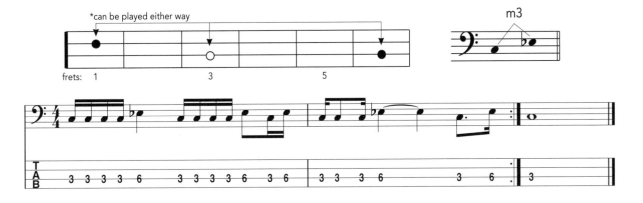

Track 134

Major Third

Track 135

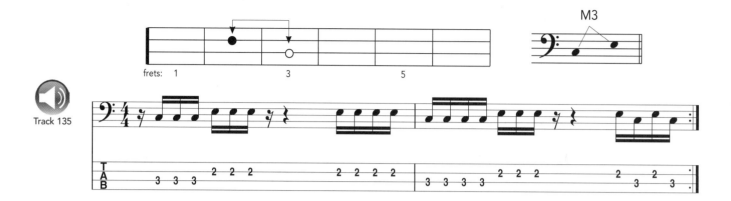

Perfect Fourth

A *fourth* is called "perfect" because it remains the same distance from the tonic whether it's found within a major or a minor scale.

Track 136

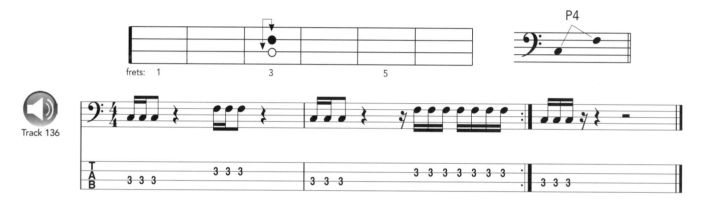

Augmented Fourth or Diminished Fifth

Augmented means to "raise one half step"; diminished means to "lower one half step."

Track 137

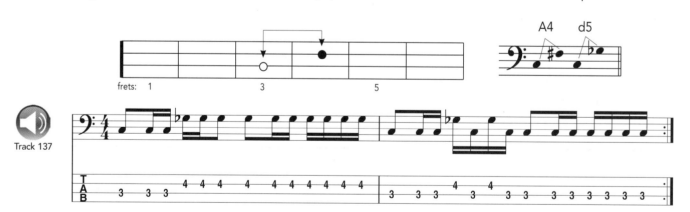

Perfect Fifth

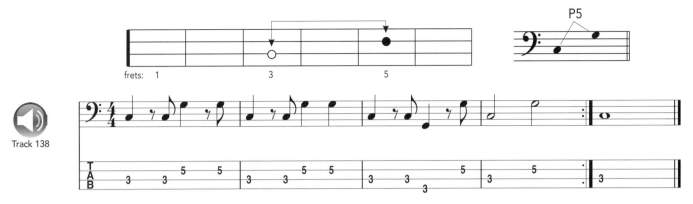

Track 138

Augmented Fifth or Minor Sixth

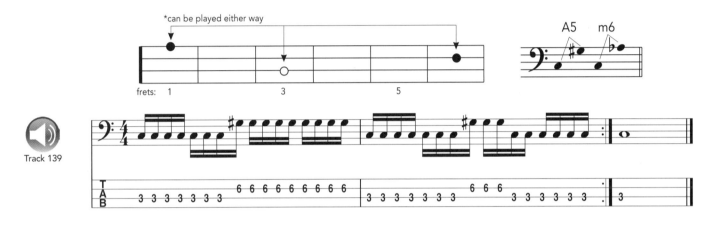

Track 139

Major Sixth

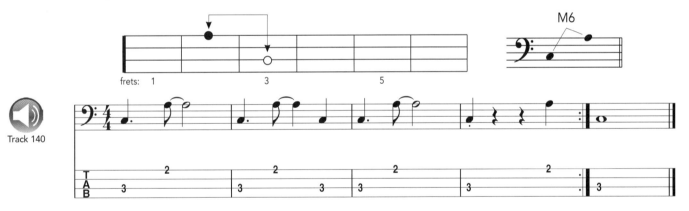

Track 140

Minor Seventh

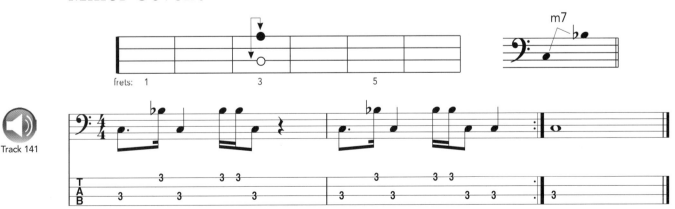

Track 141

Major Seventh

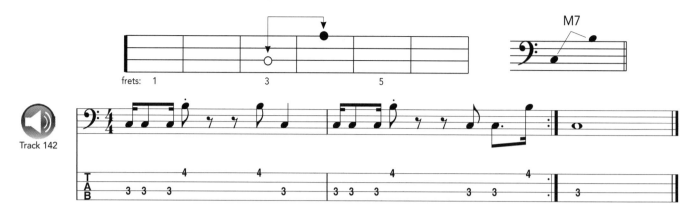

Track 142

Octave

Track 143

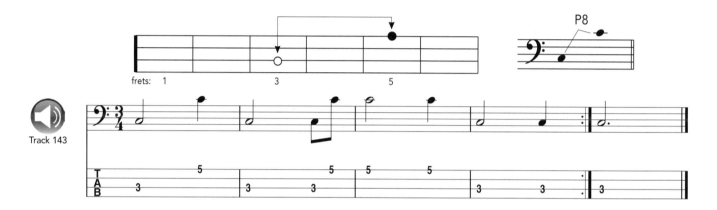

The Shuffle Feel

The **shuffle feel** is a very common element of rock, blues, pop, and jazz music. It uses a new rhythmic value called a "triplet."

By now, you know that a quarter note divided into two equal parts is two eighth notes. And a quarter note divided into four equal parts is four sixteenth notes. But a quarter note divided into three equal parts? This is an **eighth-note triplet**:

Triplets are beamed together with a number 3. To count a triplet, simply say the word "tri-pl-et" during one beat. Tap your foot to the beat, and count out loud:

count: 1   2   tri - pl - let   4   tri - pl - let   tri - pl - let   3   4   1   2   &   tri - pl - let   4

Shuffle rhythm can be derived from a triplet rhythm by inserting a rest in the middle of the triplet, or by combining the first two eighth notes of the triplet into a quarter. The result is like a triplet with a silent middle eighth note.

Once you get the hang of this "bouncy" feel, you'll never forget it...

Doug's Blues

Shuffle notation can be hard to read. So instead, you'll often see straight eighth notes with the word "swing" or ($\sqcap = \overset{3}{\sqcap}$) written at the beginning of the song. This tells you to swing, or shuffle, all eighth notes.

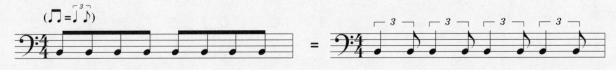

Shuffle Head

► Pay close attention to the feel on this one.

Key Review

Track 146

When we see that the notes of a particular song come from a certain scale, we say that the song is **in the key** of that scale. For instance, if the notes of a song all come from the C major scale, we say that the song is in the key of C major.

Try playing the C major scale, but change the order of the notes. Begin and end your improvisation on the note C. Notice how the scale seems to be "at rest" when you arrive at C? This is because the note C is the root, or **tonic**—the note around which the key revolves.

Most major keys—except C major—contain sharped or flatted notes. Instead of writing these out as they occur, a **key signature** is used at the beginning of each line of music to tell you:

- What notes should be played sharp or flat throughout a song.
- The song's key (scale)

For example, the key of G major contains F♯, so its key signature will have a sharp on the F-line. This tells you to play all F notes as F♯ (unless, of course, you see a natural sign). This is what the scale would look like.

This table shows all the major keys and their corresponding flats or sharps.

Key	Number of Flats	Name of Flats	Key	Number of Sharps	Name of Sharps
C	0		C	0	
F	1	B♭	G	1	F♯
B♭	2	B♭, E♭	D	2	F♯, C♯
E♭	3	B♭, E♭, A♭	A	3	F♯, C♯, G♯
A♭	4	B♭, E♭, A♭, D♭	E	4	F♯, C♯, G♯, D♯
D♭	5	B♭, E♭, A♭, D♭, G♭	B	5	F♯, C♯, G♯, D♯, A♯
G♭	6	B♭, E♭, A♭, D♭, G♭, C♭	F♯	6	F♯, C♯, G♯, D♯, A♯, E♯

The Cycle of Fifths

You can also use the cycle of fifths to learn or memorize your key signatures. As you go clockwise around the circle, you move up by fifths. Interestingly, each new key along the circle has one more sharp (or one less flat) than the previous. Using our knowledge of intervals, moving up in fifths, helps us find our keys.

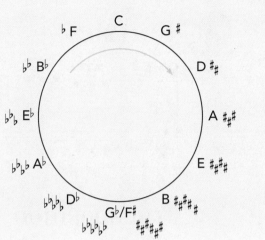

Let's practice reading in some major keys.

Track 147

Cruisin'

key of G

Track 148

Midnight

key of D

Try to figure out what key this is in by looking at the table of key signatures or the cycle of fifths.

Pottsie

Transposition

Sometimes, you'll need to play a song in a different key than what it was originally written in—perhaps a key that's more comfortable for you, your band, your singer, etc. Changing the key of a song is called **transposition.** Try playing the following simple tune—"Yankee Doodle"—in the keys below. The transposition has already been done for you.

Key of D

Key of C

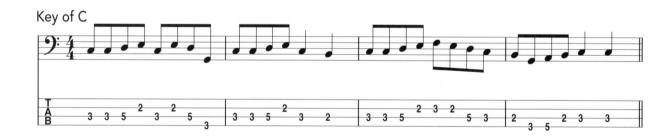

Key of E

66

The Relative Minor

One easy way to learn minor keys is to relate them to their corresponding major key. It works like this: If you begin a major scale from its sixth degree, you'll find its *relative minor* scale. The relative minor, since it uses all the same notes as the major scale, also uses the exact same key signature.

For example, play a C major scale and count up to the sixth degree, A. Now play the scale starting from this note. This is the relative minor—the same notes, just played in different order, with a different emphasis. The order in which the notes are played results in a different sound.

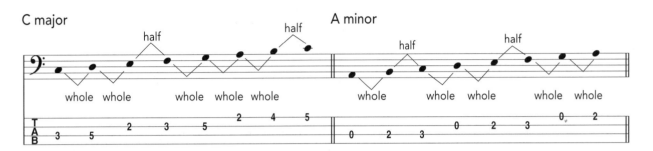

This table shows the major keys, their relative minors, and the number of flats or sharps.

Major Key	Relative Minor Key	Number of Flats	Major Key	Relative Minor Key	Number of Sharps
C	A minor	0	C	A minor	0
F	D minor	1	G	E minor	1
B♭	G minor	2	D	B minor	2
E♭	C minor	3	A	F♯ minor	3
A♭	F minor	4	E	C♯ minor	4
D♭	B♭ minor	5	B	G♯ minor	5
G♭	E♭ minor	6	F♯	D♯ minor	6

Let's play some songs in minor keys.

Track 152

Minor Issue

This song is based in the key of E minor.

Guilty

Track 153

key of E minor

Three Times

Track 154

► This one's in D minor.

Ghost Notes

Ghost notes (sometimes called "dead notes") are percussive noises created by muting or deadening the string with the left hand while plucking with the right. They are notated using an "x" instead of a notehead.

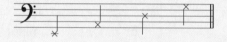

Can you guess the minor key being used here?

Casper

Track 155

Chord Theory

Track 156

Understanding chords is an essential part of playing bass. This means knowing both what a chord is *and* what to play if you see a chord symbol in a piece of music. Chord symbols will be easy to master now that you've learned the major and minor scales and their intervals.

Remember: A **note** is one single pitch, an **interval** is two different pitches, and a **chord** is three or more different pitches sounded simultaneously.

Triad

A **triad** is the basic structure of most chords and is an important building block for bass lines. A triad consists of the root, third, and fifth of a scale. Let's take a look at a few major scales and find the triad within.

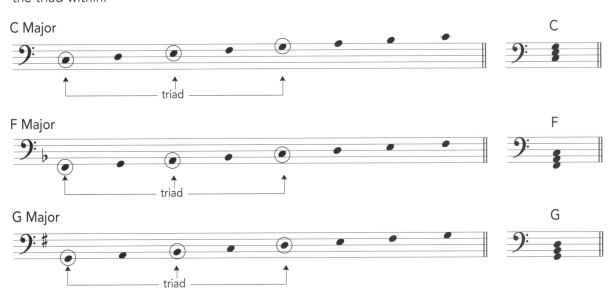

Now let's go over a few minor scales and find the triad within.

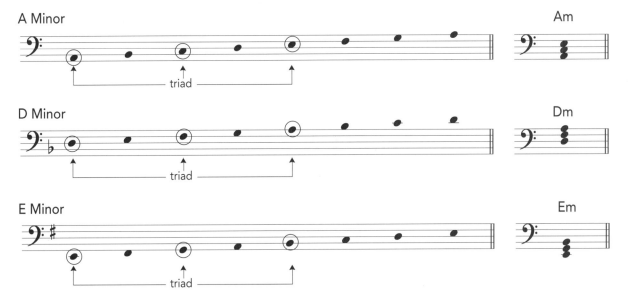

As a bassist, your job is to outline the chords—playing the notes one at a time—while other instruments such as piano or guitar play the actual chords above. Chords played one note at a time are called *arpeggios*. Let's play some arpeggios outlining major chords.

Chord symbols—such as "F" or "G"—are a form of musical shorthand, used in place of writing out the full chord name, like "F major" or "G major." When you see a single note name in a chart, it implies a major triad.

Major Triads

Track 157

► Start the G and C triads with the 2nd finger of your left hand.

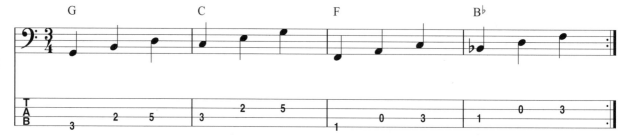

Now we'll add the octave to our major triads.

Major Triads & Octaves

Track 158

Are you ready to move on to minor? Chord symbols for minor triads are labeled with an "m" after the note—for instance, Fm or Gm.

Minor Triads

Track 159

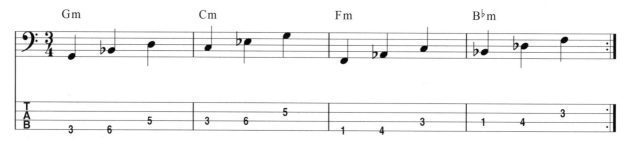

Now add the octave to our minor triads.

Minor Triads & Octaves

Track 160

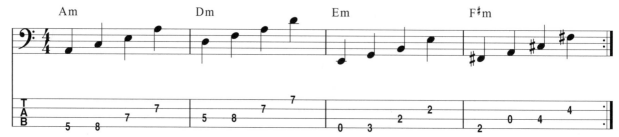

Let's combine our major and minor triads into progressions. The single element that is different between a major and minor triad is the third. A third, as you've already learned in our interval study, can be either major or minor.

Track 161

Two, Five to One

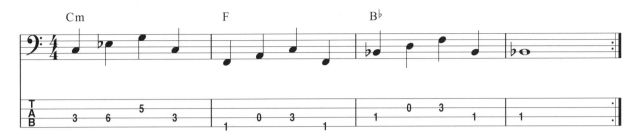

To see how triads work in bass lines, we'll try a few songs.

Track 162

Old Time

Slides

Slides are a type of articulation; they can add variety and interest to your bass lines. To play a slide like the ones shown, pluck the first note, and then sound the second note by sliding the same left-hand finger up or down along the string. (The second note is not picked.)

Track 163

Sliding

Track 164

Bluesy Groove

► This one's a stretch!

Adding The Seventh

The next step to understanding chord theory is adding the *seventh* to a chord. It's quite simple; when you see a chord labeled "maj7," it means the chord is built using the root, third, fifth, and seventh of a major scale.

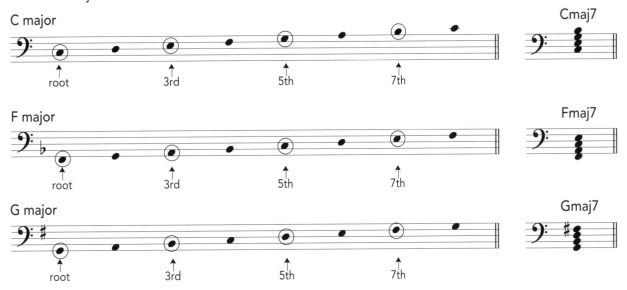

The same theory works for minor chords; when you see a chord labeled "m7," it means the chord is built using the root, third, fifth, and seventh of a minor scale.

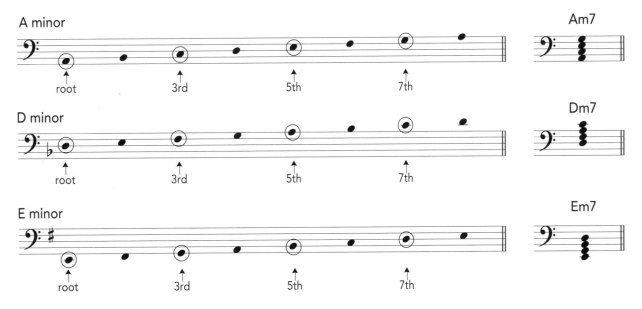

Let's play through some major seventh arpeggios, outlining the chords with the root, third, fifth, and seventh.

Track 165

Major Sevenths

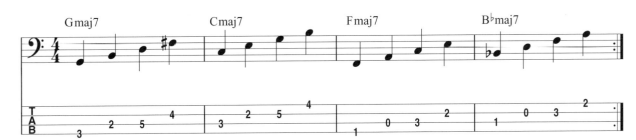

Now let's outline minor seventh chords.

Minor Sevenths

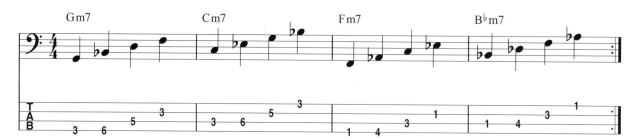

When you're ready, let's combine major and minor seventh chords into some progressions. Keep in mind, the difference between these two chord types is the third and seventh intervals—in a major seventh chord, both intervals are major; in a minor seventh chord, both are minor.

Seven & Seven

Track 167

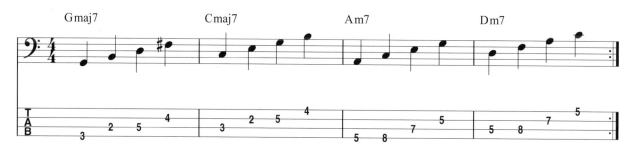

As a bassist, your job is to hold down the bottom end and to groove, so when playing over chords, you might not always play *every* note of a chord; for instance, sometimes you might play just the root. Nevertheless, understanding your options gives you creative choices and will add to the overall musicality of your bass lines.

Busy Ballad

Track 168

► Remember to read ahead!

1st and 2nd Endings

The next song has a **1st** and **2nd ending** (indicated by brackets and the numbers "1 and 2"). The first time through the song, play the 1st ending, up until the repeat sign, and then return to the beginning of the song. The second time through the song, skip the 1st ending and jump to the 2nd ending, playing until the end.

Track 169

Jamaican Beach

Chord Overview

Let's break down what we've learned about chords with a few simple formulas. These are shown in the key of C.

Chord Symbol	Scale	Intervals
C	Major	Root–M3–P5
Cm	Minor	Root–m3–P5
Cmaj7	Major	Root–M3–P5–M7
Cm7	Minor	Root–m3–P5–m7

The Dominant Scale

Track 170

One more scale to learn! This one is easy and very common. It's called the **dominant scale**; basically, it's the same as a major scale except that you flatten the seventh interval by a half step, making it a minor seventh. Let's take a closer look.

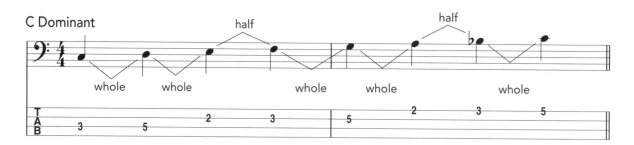

Notice the formula: whole–whole–half–whole–whole–half–whole.

Let's take a look at some more dominant scales.

Track 171

Dominant chords are famous for their unresolved sound and are used in all styles of music. Before we move onto a song, let's take a look at the dominant chord. It's built from the root, third, fifth, and seventh of a dominant scale. A dominant chord is labeled by putting a "7" after the root, such as C7 or G7.

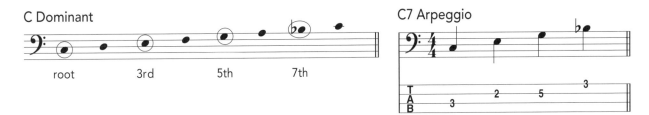

C Dominant

root   3rd   5th   7th

C7 Arpeggio

Track 172

Blue Dominant

F7

B♭7   F7

C7   B♭7   F7   C7

This song uses more than just dominant chords; listen to how the dominant chord (E♭7) wants to resolve.

Track 173

Jazzmine

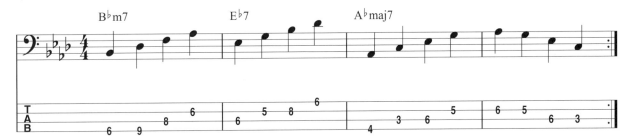

B♭m7   E♭7   A♭maj7

12/8 Time

Reading in 12/8 time is a little tricky. There are 12 eighth notes in every measure, but they're typically grouped into four sets of three. This can feel like 4/4, but with three eighth notes per one beat, which gives it a swinging feel.

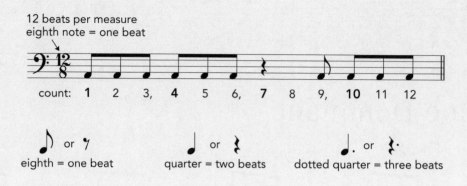

Let's try a 12/8 blues tune to help you get the feel for this new time signature.

Track 174

Chicago Shuffle

▶ Count aloud to keep the feel.

Another common time signature with this feel is **6/8**. To get a handle on this count, cut a 12/8 measure in half. 6/8 time usually has a much quicker feel than 12/8, so listen carefully before you try this one.

Track 175

Six Pack

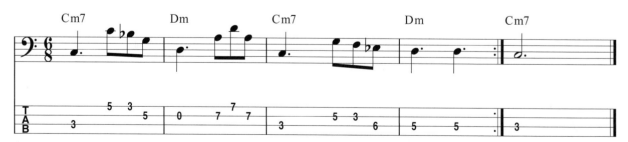

78

Slap Bass

Track 176

Slap bass is a style of playing widely used in funk, pop, soul, rock, and fusion music. It actually consists of two different techniques: the **slap**—using your thumb to slap (hit) the strings against the fingerboard; and the **pop**—using your index or middle finger to pull (snap) the string away from the fingerboard. Becoming fluent with these techniques requires a good deal of practice. Let's break them down!

Slap

This is the most important part of the technique; it's vital that you attain a good clean sound with your thumb before you move on to the pop. Attack or "slap" the string at the end of the fingerboard with the side of your thumb (at the joint), using motion from your wrist, not your arm. Let your thumb rebound (bounce) immediately (and rotate your wrist away) to allow the note to "ring" out. Bouncing the string against the fretboard and letting the string continue to vibrate creates the sound.

For starters, practice slapping half notes on the open stings. If the string is not ringing for the full two beats, practice bouncing off the string more quickly. The letter "T" (for "thumb") is used between staff and tab notation for this style.

Track 177

Thumb Open Strings

To get a good grasp on using your thumb, try your scales using the slap. For now, let's try another song!

Track 178

Digit

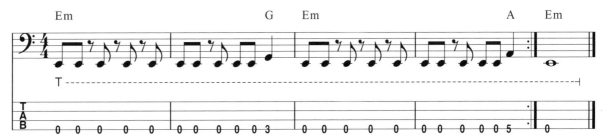

This song's a little longer, and it adds a few techniques to spice up the sound. Remember the pull-off and the hammer-on?

Drop the Hammer

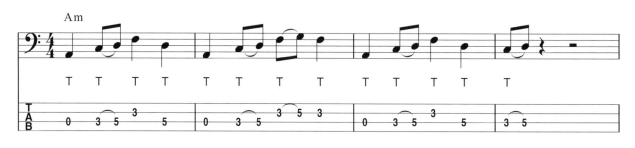

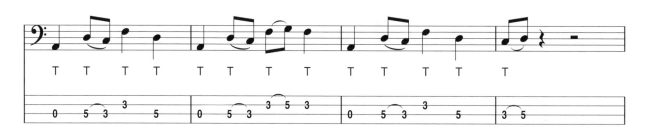

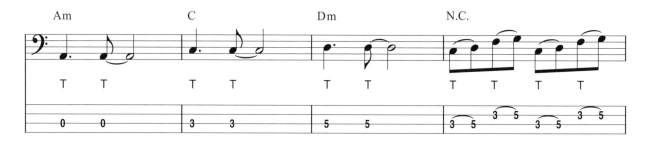

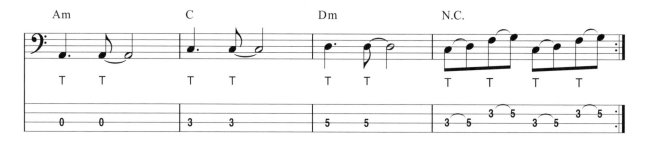

Pop

To pop a note, pull or "snap" the string away from the fretboard with your index or middle finger, again using your wrist for this motion. When released, the string will naturally rebound off the fretboard and "ring" out. Keep your right-hand fingers curled and in position to pop.

Ready to try the pop? The letter "P" is used between tab and staff notation to let you know that a note is popped.

Track 180

Pop It

Let's combine the slap and pop using octaves.

Track 181

Octagon

▶ Go slowly.

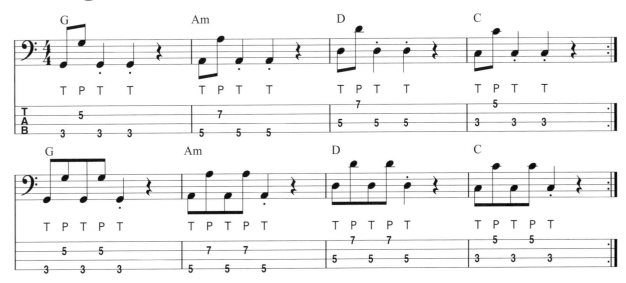

Track 182

Wake Up

Practice your slap technique by applying it to songs you would normally play fingerstyle. It's a good idea not to do this in your band, but rather on your own time, getting fluid with your thumb. This style requires finesse, so take it slow and practice your notes cleanly and precisely.

We're adding one more thing to this example, the ghost note.

Track 183

► Ghost notes are very common in slap bass.

Space Ghost!

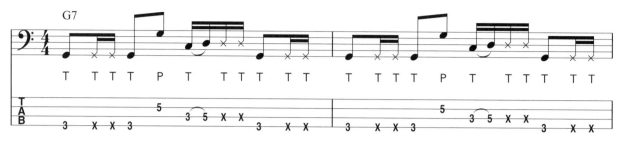

Rhythm Workout: The Thumb

Now let's review some rhythms and give your thumb a workout at the same time. As a bassist, your job is to have a great feel, and understanding rhythm gives you an advantage when it comes to grooving. So keep working at those rhythms!

A common figure is two sixteenth notes combined with an eighth rest; we'll start with both combinations of that rhythm so you get some practice. Use a thumb slap for each.

Track 184

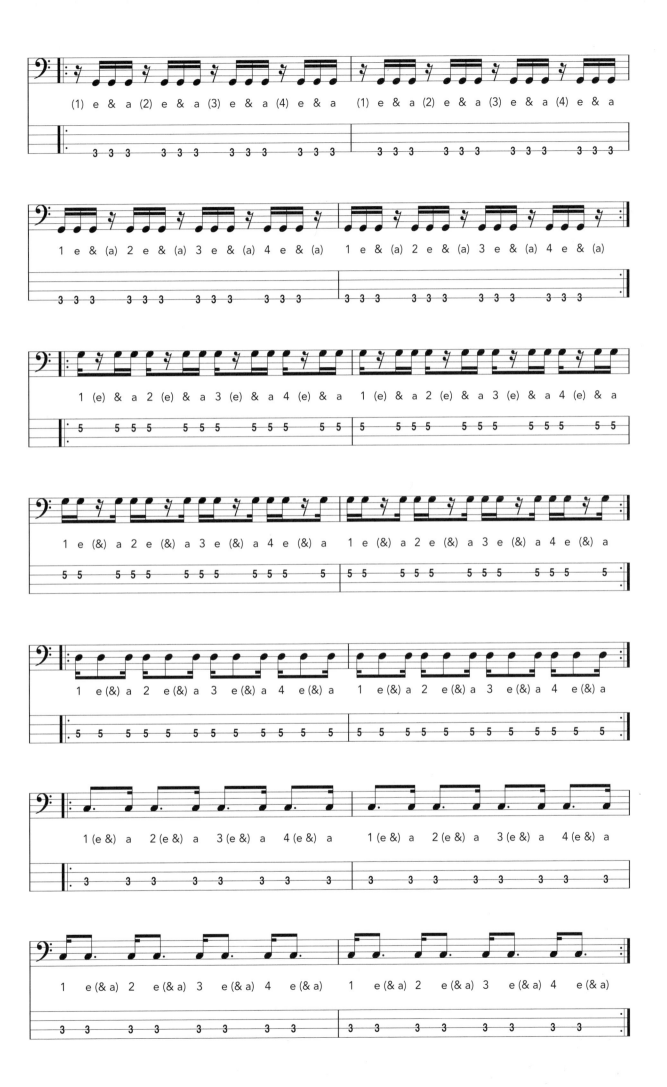

Locking In

Track 185

An important part of being a good bassist is being able to interact with a drummer. If you think about it, you are the connection between the rhythm and the harmony in your band. Your bass lines lock the grooves of the drums with the chords of the piano or guitar. That's a pretty big responsibility in the big picture of how a group sounds.

A great place to start working on your rhythm is listening to and "locking in" with the drummer. For the next examples, listen to the interaction between the bass and the bass drum.

Now listen to how the bass plays along with the bass drum and *snare*. Many bass lines alternate to the fifth or octave of the chord as the drummer strikes the snare. We'll use the same grooves as track 185, so you can get an idea of what can be done.

Ballad

Pop Rock

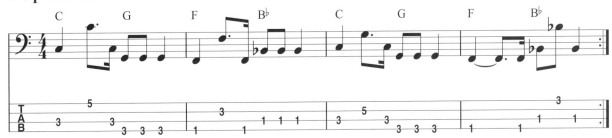

R&B

Funk

Dynamics

Another way to help the groove is by accenting certain beats within a measure or within certain sections of a song. Changing **dynamics**—the degree of loudness or softness of your notes—helps to add more life to your bass lines. Dynamic markings are located beneath the staff, slightly before the note or notes affected. These are some of the most common:

pp	*pianissimo*	very soft
p	*piano*	soft
mp	*mezzo piano*	moderately soft
mf	*mezzo forte*	medium loud
f	*forte*	loud
ff	*fortissimo*	very loud
cresc.	*crescendo*	increasing loudness
decresc. or *dim.*	*decrescendo* or *diminuendo*	decreasing loudness
>	*accent mark*	play note louder

This is how these marks would look in a piece of music.

Dynamic Duo

Putting It All Together

We're at the end—now it's time to put things together. With your knowledge of scales and chords, plus grooves and other odds 'n' ends, it's time to create your own bass lines in a practical situation.

Bass players are frequently required to read from chord symbols and to come up with bass lines on the spot. To be able to do that, one must understand chord structure and harmony, be familiar with how the bass functions in a variety of styles of music, and understand the role of a bassist, which is to create a supportive line for the melody.

Of course, every style is different; it takes time and a lot of listening to understand how the bass works in each specific idiom. For now, a sample bass line will be given to establish a basic groove, and you'll be expected to continue the same line, changing it to fit over the different chords.

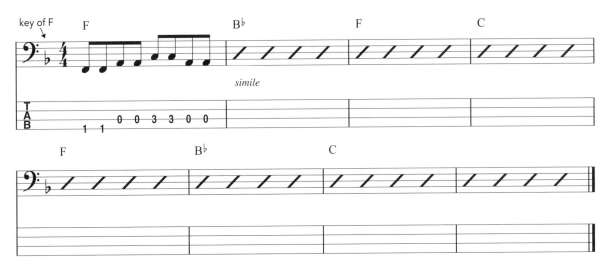

The first step is to analyze the bass line. Become familiar with it, look ahead to the chord changes, and transpose the line when needed.

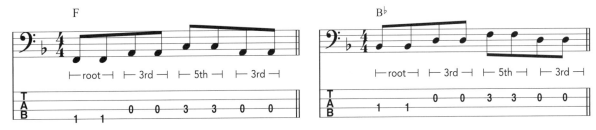

This could be what the bass line might look like when you're done.

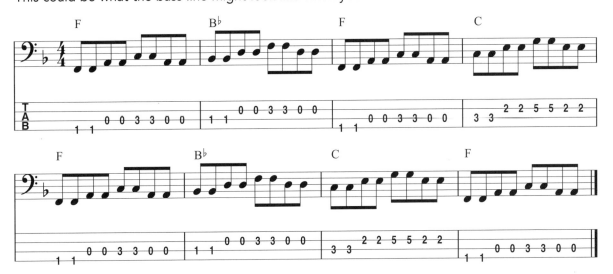

Let's start with a ballad. Watch the chord changes, and listen to the kick drum. The first four measures have the bass line written out for an example.

Track 188

Now let's try the same song with a different bass line.

Track 189

► Watch the chord changes, and work out the bass line before you start.

Ready for a blues? The first time, we'll play the bass line as a standard shuffle. The notes will be root, 3rd, 5th, and 3rd—all quarter notes—and we'll accent beats 2 and 4 to give it a better feel.

Track 190

Let's get funky now! Pay attention to the groove on this one. The same chord changes as the last song, just a different feel.

Track 191

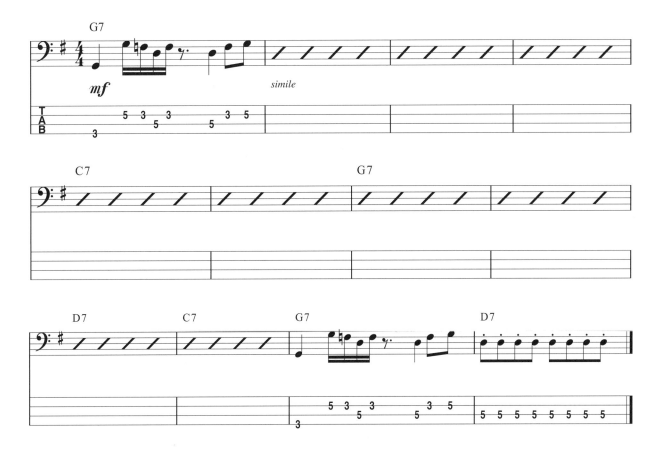

Rock, anyone? Stick to straight eighth notes the first time through. If you feel up to it, add the octave with the snare drum hits the second time.

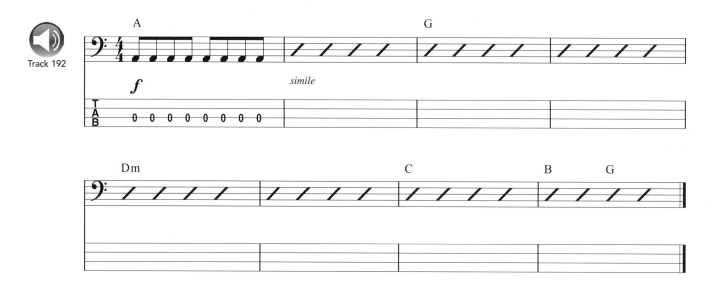

Same song, different groove. This bass line is a little more active.

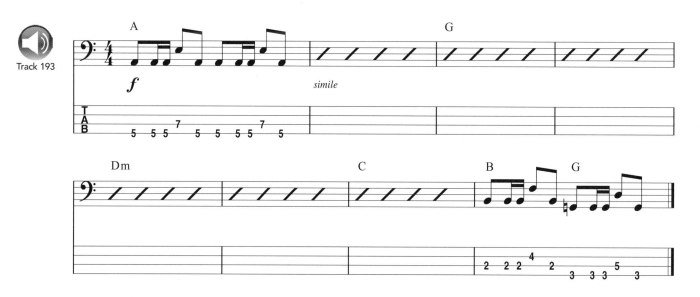

Slap style? Make sure you work out the bass line for this with all the chords ahead of time, just to be prepared.

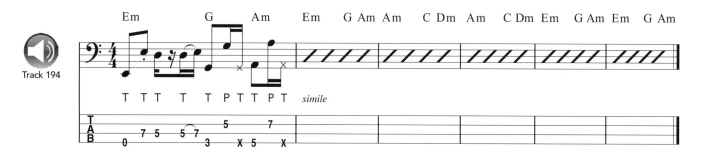

Try this song again, playing it fingerstyle without the slaps and pops—so you can appreciate the different sound that slap creates.

This song is a bossa nova. Watch the chord changes, and listen to how the bass fits in the pocket.

Track 195

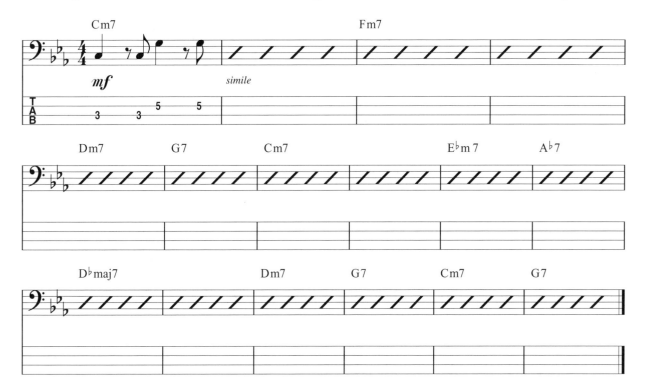

This one will be more difficult; we'll create a **walking bass** line. To "walk" a bass line, we outline the chord changes with quarter notes. There are many techniques for walking a bass line, but we'll keep it simple to start. For the first three quarter notes, play the triad of the chord, then on beat 4 use an *approach note*—a note one half step above or below the root of the chord you're approaching.

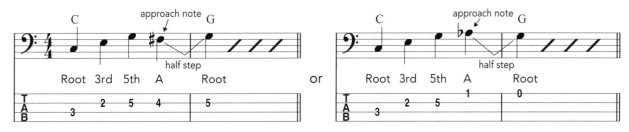

Ready? Here we go!

Track 196

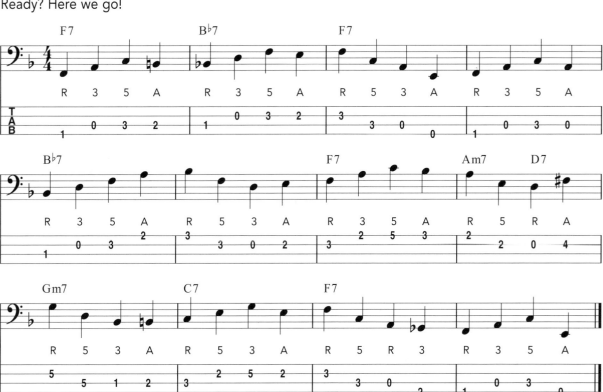

Review

Notes on the Fretboard

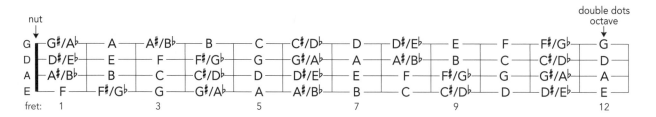

Notes in Fifth Position

Major, Minor, and Dominant Scales and Chords

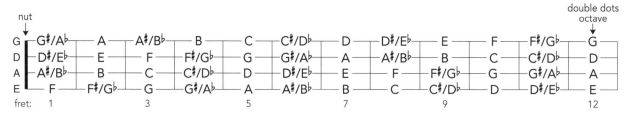

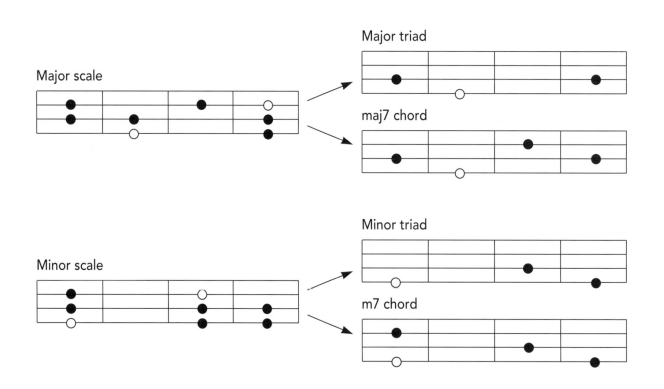

Major scale

Major triad

maj7 chord

Minor scale

Minor triad

m7 chord

How to Change a String

If you're missing a string or your strings are old and need replacing, you'll need to know how to change them. The diagram below should help. Once you've inserted the ball-end of a string at the bridge, you need to wrap the other end around the tuning peg at the headstock. To do this, first insert the string in the posthole. Then, bend it sharply to hold it in place, and begin winding. You should allow enough slack to wrap the string around the peg 3 to 4 times; any excess can be removed with a good wire cutter.

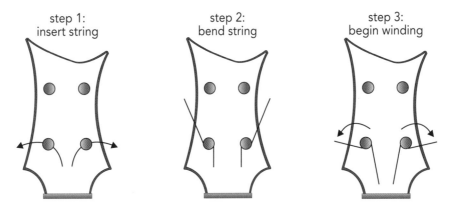

step 1:
insert string

step 2:
bend string

step 3:
begin winding

Keep in mind, new strings need to be stretched before you can expect them to hold their pitch. You can do this by playing on them awhile and tuning them up several times until each string remains in tune. (Lightly pulling on the strings one at a time, initially, can also help stretch them out.)

Adjusting the Bridge

String height (or "action") can be adjusted by raising or lowering the bridge saddles of your bass. Some saddles require a small screwdriver, but most use a small Allen wrench, which can be purchased at a hardware store if one did not come with your bass at the time of purchase.

The Truss Rod

Remember: your bass is wood (unless you purchased a graphite-neck model). With the changes of season come changes in your bass neck. Most basses have a steel rod through the neck, which can be adjusted to tighten or loosen neck tension. If you notice buzzing to be more frequent, it is a good idea to take your bass in to get the neck adjusted. If possible, watch how a professional does it so you can learn how to adjust the truss rod yourself.